Town and Village Patterns

John Corn

Advisory Teacher in Environmental Studies

ARNOLD - WHEATON

Arnold-Wheaton
A Division of E. J. Arnold & Son Limited
Parkside Lane, Leeds LS11 5TD

A subsidiary of Pergamon Press Ltd.
Headington Hill Hall, Oxford OX3 0BW

Pergamon Press Inc.
Maxwell House, Fairview Park, Elmsford, New York 10523

Pergamon Press Canada Ltd.
Suite 104, 150 Consumers Road, Willowdale, Ontario M2J 1P9

Pergamon Press (Australia) Pty. Ltd.
P.O. Box 544, Potts Point, N.S.W. 2011

Pergamon Press GmbH
Hammerweg 6, D-6242 Kronberg
Federal Republic of Germany

ISBN 0 560-26533-6

First published 1986
Printed in Great Britain by A. Wheaton & Co. Ltd.
Hennock Road, Exeter

ACKNOWLEDGEMENTS
Photograph: Bradford Bridge St. c 1905 Copyright Walter Scott Bradford
Aerial photographs: C. H. Wood Ltd., Bradford
BBC Radio Northampton
East Midlands Electricity Board
Debenhams PLC
'Dial Domestics' Hoover Service Centre, Northampton
Hoover PLC
Chronicle & Echo, Northampton
United Counties Omnibus Co. Ltd.
Asda Stores
W. G. Dyson & Sons, Bradford
Walter Ingham & Co., Shipley
Northamptonshire County Council
Telegraph & Argus Newspapers, Bradford
Illustrations by Terry Bambrook

Contents

Settlements and Services

A settlement is any place where people live. Settlements range from isolated farms to sprawling cities like London with a population of millions.

Many settlements provide services such as schools, hospitals, libraries and shops. Large settlements usually provide a much greater variety of services than small settlements.

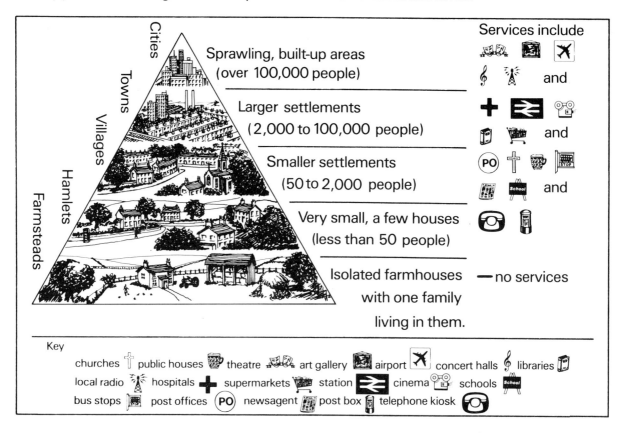

Services include

Sprawling, built-up areas (over 100,000 people)

Larger settlements (2,000 to 100,000 people)

Smaller settlements (50 to 2,000 people)

Very small, a few houses (less than 50 people)

Isolated farmhouses with one family living in them. — no services

Key

churches ✝ public houses 🍺 theatre 🎭 art gallery 🖼 airport ✈ concert halls 🎵 libraries 📖
local radio 📡 hospitals ✚ supermarkets 🛒 station 🚆 cinema 📽 schools School
bus stops 🚏 post offices (PO) newsagent 📰 post box 🛢 telephone kiosk ☎

Activities

A Look at the diagram above.

1 In which type of settlement do you live?

2 For your part of the country, write down the name of:
(a) a city (b) a town (c) a village (d) a hamlet (e) a farmstead. An Ordnance Survey map will help you.

3 Using the chart, try to estimate the population of each settlement by looking at the services it provides. Here are the population numbers for the settlements: 114,461 682 45,233 21 184 5 1,793 3 256,335. The first one is done for you.

Settlement	Services	Population
Thorpe	No services	**3**
Ashfield	✝ 🍺 (PO) ☎ 📰	
Weston	No services	
Belford	✚ 📖 🚏 🚆 🛒 ✝ School	
Welbridge	🎭 ✚ 🚆 📽 🎵	
Tindon	📖 ☎	
Bradfield	🎭 🖼 ✈ 📡 ✚ 🎵	
Hambledon	(PO) 🚏 📰 School ✝ 🍺	
Hempstead	🛒 School 📖 🚏 (PO)	

4

Look at an Ordnance Survey 1:25 000 scale map of your area. Using the key, try to identify some of the services that your local settlements provide. Make a chart like this one. Choose a variety of settlements.

Settlement	Services
Longthorn	post office
Marsden	public house, phone box

Towns provide services which are used for miles around as well as in the towns themselves. They may be centres for local newspapers and radio stations, and from which people are sent out to repair such things as washing machines, or deliver furniture.

This map shows the area covered by service engineers from the East Midlands Electricity Board based in Northampton.

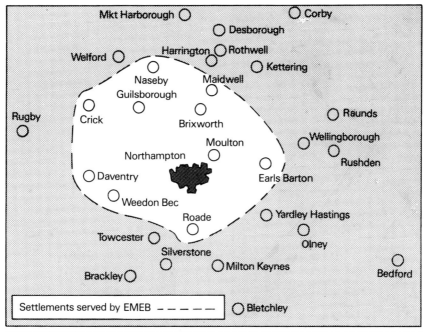

Company	Settlements served
East Midlands Electricity Board (EMEB)	Daventry, Crick, Naseby, Maidwell, Earls Barton, Roade, Weedon Bec
Chronicle & Echo	Rothwell, Kettering, Rushden, Olney, Bletchley, Brackley, Daventry, Crick
Hoover-Dial Domestics	Kettering, Wellingborough, Olney, Silverstone, Guilsborough, Maidwell
BBC Radio Northampton	Market Harborough, Corby, Bedford, Bletchley, Rugby
Debenhams	Yardley Hastings, Roade, Weedon Bec, Crick, Welford, Harrington, Earls Barton

B 1 Make an 'area of influence' map for Northampton. Copy the map above and using the information from the chart, join together places receiving the same service. Use a different coloured pencil for each service. This has already been done for the East Midlands Electricity Board.
   2 Name two settlements from the map that are best served by the five companies considered. Name two settlements that are poorly served.

Things to think about
1 What do you think are the most important services a settlement should provide?
2 What could be done for people living in farmsteads, hamlets, or small villages to provide them with basic services?

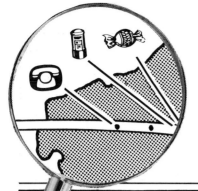

Investigating
Local Services

Life is much easier when services such as shops and schools are close by. We can find out how well served we are by measuring the distance from our homes to each amenity. The closer to each amenity we are, the better.

Yasmin and Tim live near Bradchester. They decided to see which of their homes was best served. The map shows their homes and the ten amenities which they use most.

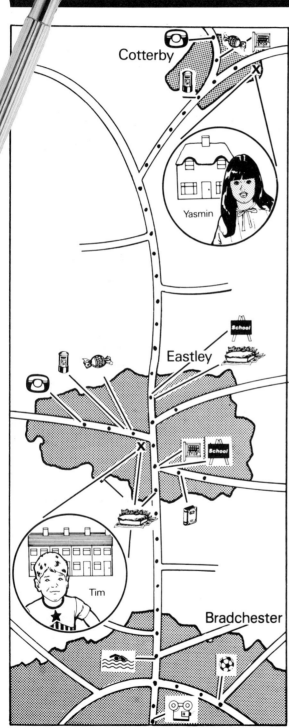

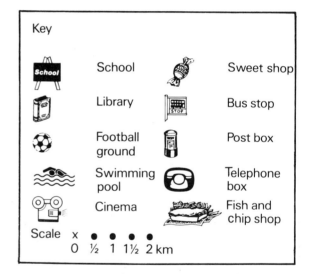

Key

School	School	Sweet shop	Sweet shop
Library	Library	Bus stop	Bus stop
Football ground	Football ground	Post box	Post box
Swimming pool	Swimming pool	Telephone box	Telephone box
Cinema	Cinema	Fish and chip shop	Fish and chip shop

Scale x ● ● ● ●
0 ½ 1 1½ 2 km

Activities

A Use the map and a copy of the chart to see whether it is Tim's or Yasmin's home that is best served. This is what you do.
1 Find out how far it is to each amenity from Yasmin's home.
2 Do this again for Tim's home. Remember that each dot on the map represents a distance of ½ km.
3 Add up the total distances for each home.
4 Who has the lowest Amenity Index, Yasmin or Tim?

Amenity	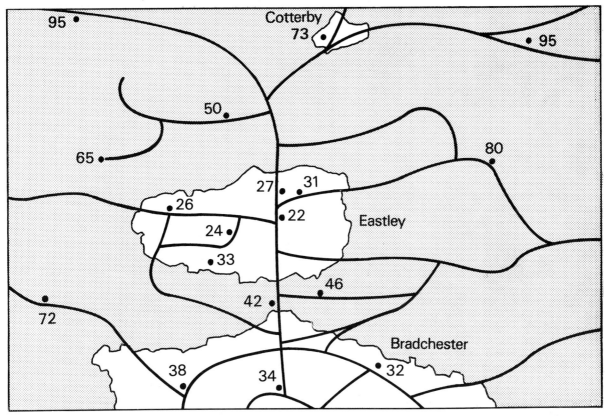										TOTAL km
Distance from Yasmin's home	$1\frac{1}{2}$						$10\frac{1}{2}$				
Distance from Tim's home	$\frac{1}{2}$						$1\frac{1}{2}$				

Everyone in Yasmin's class worked out the Amenity Index for their home. Their teacher plotted the results on a street map. This is what they found.

B **1** Which areas seem to be (a) best served? (b) worst served?

2 What disadvantages might there be to living in a well served area?

3 Work in a group to investigate your local services. Choose ten amenities but make sure that everyone in the class uses the same list. Measure the distance from home to the amenity in paces or minutes.

This is what you do.

- Work out how far it is from your home to each of the amenities in turn, and complete a chart like Yasmin and Tim.
- What is your Amenity Index?
- Collect the results for your group. Put them in order starting with the best Amenity Index (the lowest score) and ending with the worst (the highest score).
- Compare the results for your group with those for the whole class. Who is best placed for these amenities? Who is worst placed?

Town and Village Land Use

A land use study describes how every piece of land in an area is used. The following are a few of the many uses land is put to: housing, factories, shops, woodland and farming. Looking at the way in which land is used can tell us about the activities of the people in that area.

The maps and photographs below show how land use maps are made for two different areas.

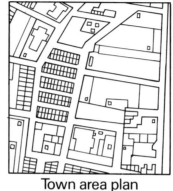
Town area plan
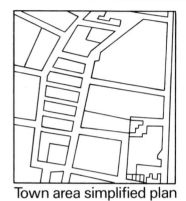
Town area simplified plan

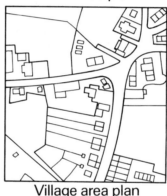
Village area plan
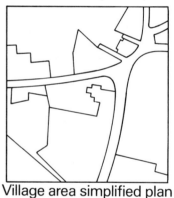
Village area simplified plan

Activities

A **1** Make a land use map for these two areas.
Trace the simplified town and village plans above. Colour in each area of land according to how you think the land is used.
Try to use this colour scheme:

Houses and gardens . . . . Red	Schools, churches,	
Industry. . . . . Black	chapels . . . . .Purple	
Shops. . . . . Blue	Farmyards and	
Fields. . . . . Green	outbuildings. . . . . .Brown	
Roads. . . . . Yellow	Other land . . . . Pencil	

2 Give each of your two maps a title and key.
3 Describe the land use in each area. Which has the most housing? Which has the most farmland? What other differences can you see?
4 In which area would you prefer to live? What are your reasons?

The greatest variety of land use can be seen in towns. Every town is different, but the overall pattern of land use is often similar.

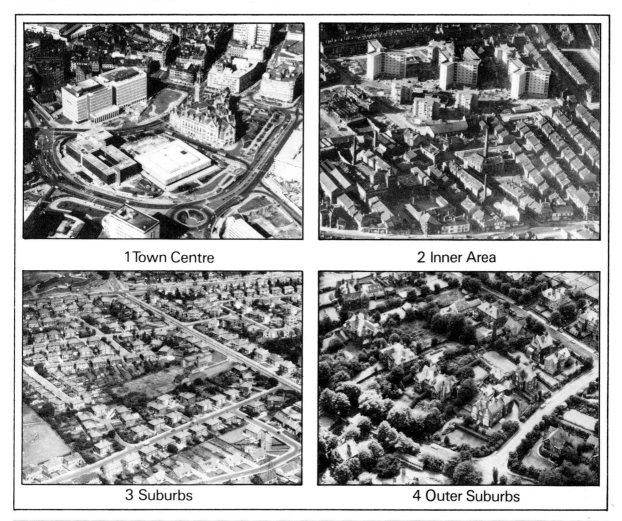

1 Town Centre

2 Inner Area

3 Suburbs

4 Outer Suburbs

B **1** Describe what you can see in each of the photographs. Think about the amount of open space and the number and size of buildings.
 2 Which zone has:
  (a) most roads?
  (b) most open space?
  (c) most shops?
  (d) most houses?
 3 In which of the four land use zones would you expect to find each of the following? You can name more than one zone if you wish.

the main shopping centre	industry
golf course	football ground
housing estates	fields
parks	cemeteries
woodland	allotments
wasteland	car parks

Things to think about
1 Why do you think most shops are found in the centre of towns?
2 Should people be allowed to build new houses on good farmland?

Investigating
Land Use in School

Make a list of all the different areas of your school. Here are a few to start you off: classrooms, corridors, store rooms.

How many have you written down – ten, fifteen, twenty perhaps? Many of these areas have something in common, for example classrooms, work spaces and libraries are all learning areas so we can say that they share the same land use. Look closely at this plan of Grove Lane Primary School.

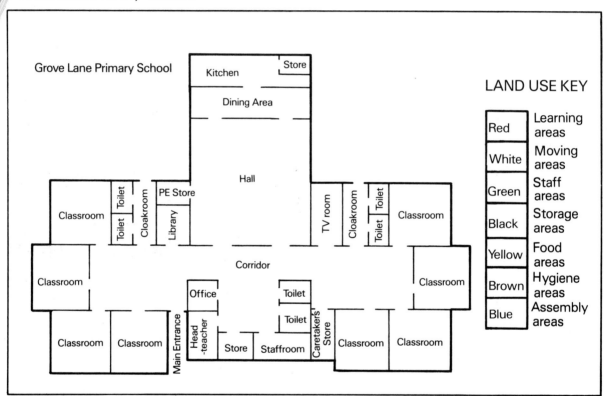

Grove Lane Primary School

Kitchen | Store
Dining Area
Hall
PE Store
Classroom | Toilet | Toilet | Cloakroom | Library
TV room | Cloakroom | Toilet | Toilet | Classroom
Corridor
Classroom
Office
Head-teacher
Main Entrance
Toilet
Toilet
Caretakers Store
Classroom
Classroom | Classroom | Store | Staffroom | Classroom | Classroom

LAND USE KEY

Red	Learning areas
White	Moving areas
Green	Staff areas
Black	Storage areas
Yellow	Food areas
Brown	Hygiene areas
Blue	Assembly areas

Activities

1 On a copy of this plan colour in each area of the school according to its land use, as shown in the key.
2 Make a list of all the land uses in the school in order, starting with the one that takes up the most space.
3 Which land use takes up the most space?
4 Which land use takes up the least space?
5 Carry out an investigation in your school to see how land is used. On an outline plan, record land use in every part of the school. Later, using the key above, colour in your plan.
6 List the land uses in your school, starting with the one that takes up the most space. How does their order compare with that of Grove Lane Primary School?

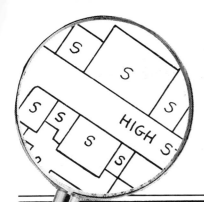

Investigating
Local Land Use

As in school, your local area contains many different land uses. The school has different land uses so that it can run smoothly. The same is true for the community it serves. People need houses in which to live, shops for food, and places to work and relax. Each of these activities uses land. A group of children decided to investigate the local land use near their school. They walked around the area noting down what each building and plot of land was used for, marking it on a large scale map. This is their land use map for Manningley.

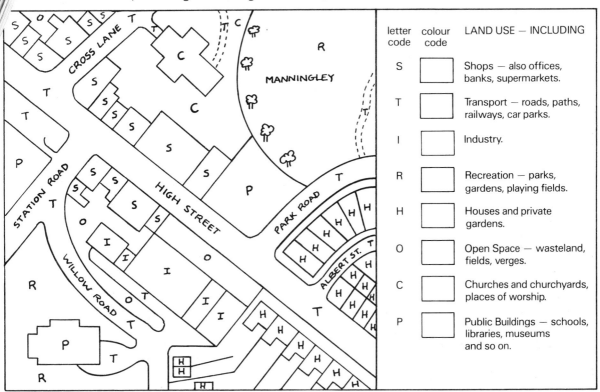

letter code	colour code	LAND USE — INCLUDING
S		Shops — also offices, banks, supermarkets.
T		Transport — roads, paths, railways, car parks.
I		Industry.
R		Recreation — parks, gardens, playing fields.
H		Houses and private gardens.
O		Open Space — wasteland, fields, verges.
C		Churches and churchyards, places of worship.
P		Public Buildings — schools, libraries, museums and so on.

Activities

1 Look at the key. Decide on a colour code.
2 On a copy of the map colour in the land use, using the key.
3 Describe the most important land uses in the area.

Things to think about

1 In which of the four land use zones of a town do you think Manningley is situated? (Is it the town centre, the inner area, the suburbs or the outer suburbs?)
2 What problems are there when shops, industry and houses are built close together?
3 Think about the land use in your area. Are there any things you would like to change? If so, with what would you replace them?

Shopping Around

Everyone needs food, clothes, furniture and other goods. Where there are many people, there is a greater need for these things. Therefore there are a greater number and variety of shops in large towns than in small villages. This map shows which shops are found in a number of different-sized settlements.

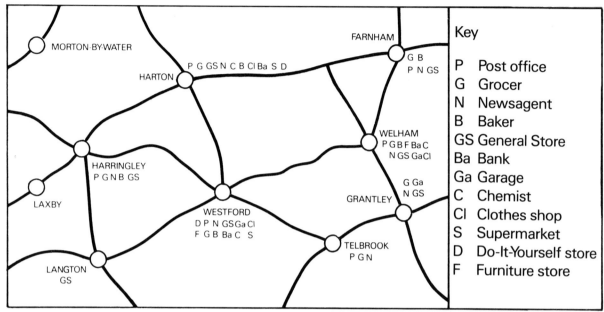

Activities

A
  1 Look carefully at the map and key. Write down the names of all the settlements on the map.
  2 List the shops found at each settlement.
  3 Next to each settlement, say whether you think it is a town, village or hamlet.
  4 What do you notice about the type of settlement and the number of shops?

Very few people do all their shopping in one place. Often a family's weekly or fortnightly food shopping is done in a supermarket. Local shops are used for things needed urgently, daily, or forgotten in the weekly shopping. Town centres have few food shops, but more clothes, furniture and electrical shops. These sell the more expensive items which we need less often.

B
  1 Copy the shopping chart and fill in your own answers.
  2 What sort of items would you buy locally?
  3 What sort of items would you buy in a town centre?
  4 Can you think of three other items that people would only buy every few years?

Items	How often I would buy them	Where I would buy them ✓	
		Local Shop	Town Centre
Bread	Every day	✓	
Jam			
Toothpaste			
Carpets			
Shampoo			
Shoes	Every 6 months		✓
Washing Machine			
Jumper			

Over the last 25 years there has been a large increase in the population of some villages, and yet a drop in the number of village shops. Can you suggest why?

Village shops cannot stock a wide range of goods, due to a lack of space. They cannot buy their stock in bulk, so they have to charge higher prices than supermarkets. Look at these tables based on a shopping list for one meal. They show the prices charged and the choice available for seven items.

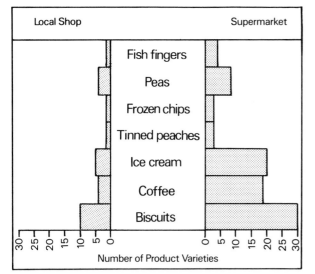

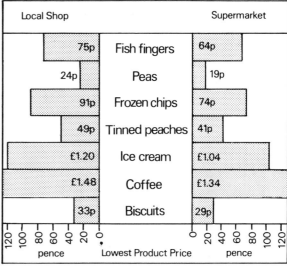

C 1 Which shop do you think has the best chance of offering exactly what shoppers want?
2 Which is the cheapest place to shop? How much will you save if you buy everything on the shopping list here?
3 Work out how many hours each week the village shop and the supermarket are open.
4 Write a few sentences about each type of shop. Which seems to be the most useful for the average shopper?
5 Can you think of any service the village shop might offer the customer that a supermarket does not offer?

HOURS OF OPENING

MON	9·00 – 1·00	2·00 – 6·00
TUE	9·00 – 1·00	4·00 – 6·00
WED	9·00 – 1·00	2·00 – 6·00
THUR	9·00 – 1·00	2·00 – 6·00
FRI	9·00 – 1·00	2·00 – 6·00
SAT	9·00 – 1·00	2·00 – 5·30
SUN	8·00 – 12·30	CLOSED

CLOSED

Local Shop		Supermarket
3	Staff	400 inc. part-time
	Hours open	
None	Car parking	for 650
550	Number of product varieties	27,000
No	Home and hardware section	Yes
None	Toilets	Yes

SHOPPING HOURS

Mon	9·00 a.m. to 5·30 p.m.
Tues	9·00 a.m. to 6·00 p.m.
Wed	9·00 a.m. to 8·00 p.m.
Thur	9·00 a.m. to 8·30 p.m.
Fri	9·00 a.m. to 8·30 p.m.
Sat	8·30 a.m. to 5·00 p.m.

Things to think about
1 'Support your local shop.' This slogan is from a campaign run several years ago. Do you think that we should do this?
2 Do you think it would be a good or bad thing if local shops closed? How would this affect old people and people without cars?

Investigating
Supermarkets

Supermarkets are an important part of modern life. Over 15,000 people visit this supermarket each week; yet the town in which it is situated has a population of only 17,000. So, where do the shoppers come from, and why do they come here?

The answer can be found by discovering a little about the people who use supermarkets.

When conducting a survey at a local supermarket, here are some things you should aim to find out:

● How far people travel to shop there.
● What sort of transport they use.
● How often people shop there.
● Why people shop at the supermarket.
● If the prices are cheaper there than at the local shops.

You will need to interview a number of shoppers. Write down the questions you want to ask them. Page 30 gives an example of a questionnaire.

One school did such a survey and asked 58 shoppers where they lived and what method of transport they had used to get to the supermarket. The information was recorded on the results matrix.

Where do you live?	How do you travel?		
	Walk	Bus	Car
Telbrook	O	O	III
Harton	O	I	IHT
Harringley	O	O	IHT
Langton	O	O	III
Westford	III	IHT I	IHT IHT IHT IHT IHT
Welham	O	O	IHT
Grantley	O	O	II

Activities

A 1 How do most people travel to the supermarket?
   2 Why should even those people living close to the supermarket avoid walking?
   3 What is the disadvantage of going by bus?

The results from the matrix were plotted on a map of the area. All the information for Westford has been filled in. The other places have been left blank.

The pupils also asked shoppers how often they went to the supermarket. To help them understand the answers the shoppers were also asked why they used the supermarket instead of their local shops.

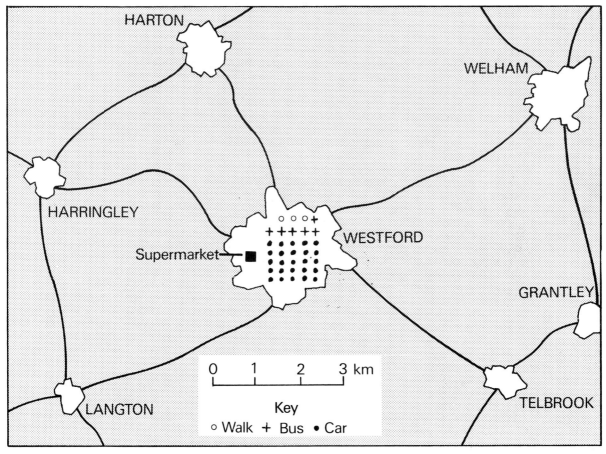

B Copy the map and for each settlement mark in how the shoppers travel to the supermarket. Use the key on the map. Westford has been done for you.

C 1 How often do most people shop at the supermarket?
2 Why do you think that few people shop every day?
3 Why do most people like shopping here?
4 Can you think of any other reasons why people might shop here?
5 Find out the prices of the same ten items in a local shop and in the supermarket. Which is the most expensive? What is the difference in price?

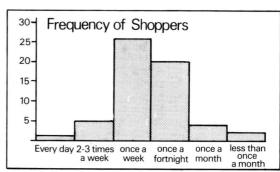

Why do people shop here and not locally?
People gave the following reasons:

Because it is convenient	7
The prices are low	26
Lots to choose from	13
Pleasant surroundings	6
All my needs are under one roof	4
Easy parking	2

Patterns of Transport by Car

The number of people using the roads constantly changes. Here are two photographs of the same road, taken only two hours apart.

What do you notice about the amount of traffic in each photograph? When do you think they were taken?

This chart shows the number of people using a main road into town over a twelve-hour period.

People using London Road between 6 am and 6 pm.												
	6 am-7 am	7 am-8 am	8 am-9 am	9 am-10 am	10 am-11 am	11 am-12 noon	12 noon-1 pm	1 pm-2 pm	2 pm-3 pm	3 pm-4 pm	4 pm-5 pm	5 pm-6 pm
Workers	300	500	800	100	100	150	200	200	100	200	600	800
Shoppers	10	30	100	200	300	250	400	200	300	200	200	50
School Children	—	100	200	—	—	—	100	50	—	200	100	—

Activities

A **1** Work out the total number of people using the road each hour.

2 Between which hours is the road busiest? Why do you think this is so?

3 When is the road quietest? Why should this be?

4 Draw a bar graph to show the total number of road users per hour, over this twelve-hour period.

People need to travel into and around towns at different times of the day. Bus timetables are drawn up with this in mind. By looking at them we can see when transport is most needed.

Times	Services		
	Number 468 bus	Number 469 bus	Number 702 bus
6 am-7 am	12	8	4
7 am-8 am	12	12	8
8 am-9 am	12	12	8
9 am-10 am	12	8	4
10 am-11 am	4	4	4
11 am-12 noon	4	4	4
12 noon-1 pm	8	8	4
1 pm-2 pm	4	4	4
2 pm-3 pm	4	4	4
3 pm-4 pm	12	8	4
4 pm-5 pm	12	12	8
5 pm-6 pm	12	12	8

This table shows the number of buses using the main road into town.

B **1** How many buses travel along the road between (a) 8 am and 9 am? (b) 10 am and 11 am? Account for the differences.

2 Draw a bar graph to show the number of buses using this road each hour from 6 am until 6 pm.

3 How does this graph compare with the graph you drew previously showing the total number of road users?

The A692 is a long road which links a major town with many other smaller settlements. Between 8 am and 9 am traffic is building up and flowing into the town. Not all of the road is busy with traffic.

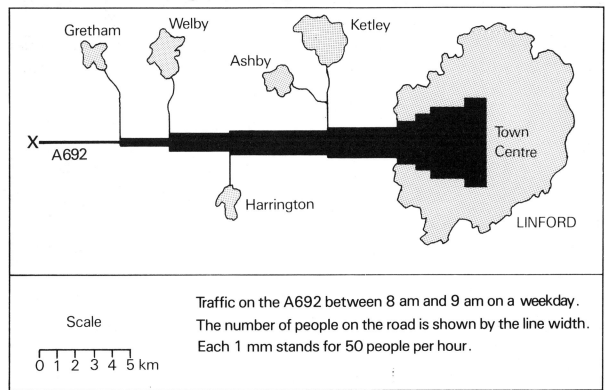

Scale

0 1 2 3 4 5 km

Traffic on the A692 between 8 am and 9 am on a weekday.
The number of people on the road is shown by the line width.
Each 1 mm stands for 50 people per hour.

C 1 What happens to the amount of traffic on the main road each time another road joins it?
2 What do you notice about the amount of people using the road when it crosses the town boundary?
3 Where do you think the fastest and slowest parts of the road are, on a journey from point X to the town centre? Explain your answer.
4 Copy and complete the line graph to show the build up of road users on the A692 between 8 am and 9 am. The graph has been started for you.
5 Estimate how many people from Welby join the main road between 8 am and 9 am.

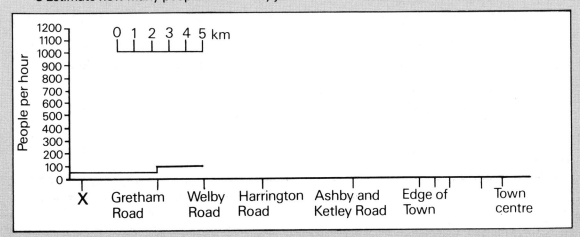

Things to think about
What do you think could be done to speed up the movement of traffic at busy periods? What has been done in your town?

Patterns of Transport by Bus

Almost everyone needs transport to reach services such as shops, libraries or leisure centres. People living close to them may walk, but for people living in villages and town suburbs walking may be impossible because of the distances involved. Many people may not be able to afford the expense of a car. As bus services are planned to serve areas of high population, even large villages may only have a few buses each day and small villages none at all!

Activities

A Look at this bus network map. The total population of the area is 250,000.
1 How many people live in the settlements served by the bus company?
2 In what kind of settlement is the need for cars highest?
3 Draw a network map for your area.

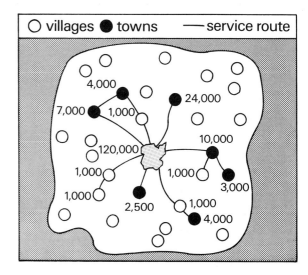

Bus companies try to make a profit. Some of their income is provided by the council, the rest comes from fares paid by the passengers. Bus companies can increase their incomes by serving areas of high population. In such areas more people will use the buses and pay more in fares. In rural areas, where the population is low, the fares collected may not even be enough to cover the cost of fuel for the bus, let alone the wages of the driver and conductor, resulting in the bus company making a loss. Here are the details of the 687 bus service from Easton to Linford.

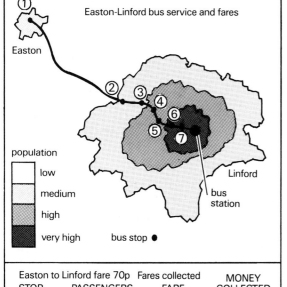

Easton-Linford bus service and fares

population
low
medium
high
very high   bus stop ●

B **1** Copy and complete the chart to find out how much money was collected on this service.
2 If it cost £16 to run the bus from Easton to Linford, did the service make a profit, loss, or break even?
3 Which stop was the most profitable and which the least? In what sort of population areas were they?

Easton to Linford fare 70p		Fares collected	
STOP	PASSENGERS	FARE	MONEY COLLECTED
1	2	70p	£1.40
2	3	50p	
3	4	45p	
4	7	40p	
5	8	35p	
6	14	30p	
7	7	25p	
		Total	_____

Service No.	324	324	324	324	326	326	324	324
Depart Spratton (Brixworth Rd)	06.30	07.41	09.05	13.28	17.04	18.43	20.10	21.30
Arrive Northampton (Bus Station)	07.08	08.20	09.48	14.02	17.27	19.06	20.33	21.53
Service No.	326	326	324	324	324	324	324	324
Depart Northampton (Bus Station)	06.03	06.54	12.20	14.50	16.25	17.40	19.40	21.00
Arrive Spratton (Brixworth Rd)	06.26	07.17	12.59	15.29	17.04	18.19	20.10	21.30

Tuesday Service Spratton-Northampton
Northampton-Spratton   Services 324 and 326

UNITED COUNTIES
a NATIONAL bus company

C   Study the timetable for the Tuesday bus service from the village of Spratton to Northampton and return.

1 How many buses are there each way?

2 Which parts of the day are best served? Why do you think this is?

Sarah Davis

"I have an appointment at the dentist's in town at 11.30. I should be free to return home at 11.45."

George Miller

"I start work at the factory at 07.30 and finish at 16.30."

Farah Aktar

"I am going to the cinema. The film starts at 19.30 and ends at 22.20."

John Scott

"I want to go away for the day by train. It leaves the station in town at 07.15 and returns at 21.15."

3 Look at the travel needs of these four villagers from Spratton. Can everyone get to their appointments and return to the village by bus?

4 Which bus should each person catch to travel into Northampton?

5 How long does Sarah have to wait in Northampton before her appointment? Is this a shorter or longer time than George will have to wait?

6 When is the last bus from Northampton on a Tuesday? By how much will Farah and John miss this?

7 What is the longest interval between buses during the day?

8 What can you say about the bus service to Spratton?

Things to think about

Do you think that there should be a law to force bus companies to provide more services to villages, at a reasonable cost?

Investigating
Traffic Flows

People travel into towns for a variety of reasons. They might travel to work, to shop or for entertainment. The time at which they travel affects the amount and type of traffic on the roads. Traffic flow on a main road will not be the same all along its length; certain parts of it will be busier than others.

To investigate the traffic flow on a main road near your school, here is what you do.

Count cars, buses, cycles and motor cycles travelling towards town on a chart like those below. You need to conduct a twenty-minute survey at three separate points along the road. BE CAREFUL NEAR THE ROAD. Once back in school work out the number of road users.

Assume that:

each car carries 2 people
each double decker bus carries 50 people
each single decker bus carries 25 people
each cycle and motor cycle carries 1 person.

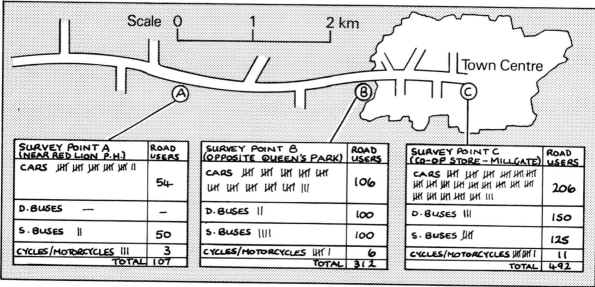

Scale 0   1   2 km

Town Centre

SURVEY POINT A (NEAR RED LION P.H.)	ROAD USERS
CARS JHT JHT JHT JHT JHT II	54
D. BUSES —	—
S. BUSES II	50
CYCLES/MOTORCYCLES III	3
TOTAL	107

SURVEY POINT B (OPPOSITE QUEEN'S PARK)	ROAD USERS
CARS JHT JHT JHT JHT JHT JHT JHT JHT JHT JHT III	106
D. BUSES II	100
S. BUSES IIII	100
CYCLES/MOTORCYCLES JHT I	6
TOTAL	312

SURVEY POINT C (CO-OP STORE – MILLGATE)	ROAD USERS
CARS JHT JHT JHT JHT JHT HTI JHT JHT JHT JHT JHT JHT JHT JHT JHT JHT JHT JHT JHT JHT III	206
D. BUSES III	150
S. BUSES JHT	125
CYCLES/MOTORCYCLES JHT JHT I	11
TOTAL	492

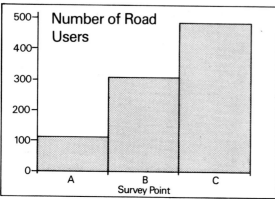

Number of Road Users

Survey Point

Activities

A **1** Where are the most road users and where are the least?

2 What happens to the amount of road users along the survey road?

3 How does the graph from your results compare with this one?

4 How will the results change if you conduct surveys at different times of the day?

The reasons why people use different types of transport are very interesting. One class conducted a survey to find out a little about the people who use the buses in their area. They visited the local bus station and interviewed at least ten people who were either waiting for, or getting off buses. If you do such a survey remember to be polite. Complete a chart like the one below.

	Interview 1	Interview 2	Interview 3	Interview 4
Where do you come from?	Ecclesfield (in Westfield)	Dington (village)	Manfley (in Westfield)	Steadford (town)
Why have you come to town?	shop	shop	work	visit friends
What fare did you pay?	40p	£1	30p	£1·20
How often do you travel by bus?	most days	weekly	every day	not often - once a month
What do you think about the bus service you use?	'they run quite often but seem expensive'	'the buses don't run often enough and are expensive'	'they are cheap and frequent'	'quite good - no complaints'

When you have finished, make a plan of the bus station. Colour bus bays for districts in your town in red, other towns in blue and villages in green. For some bus bays you may need more than one colour, if the bus stops in different settlements.

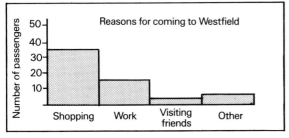

The class gathered together all the information and plotted on a map the place from where the people which they interviewed came. Did most people come from Westfield or outlying towns and villages?

B 1 Look at the bar graph. Why do most people come into town?
2 Draw a graph to show your results. How do they compare?
3 Use your results to work out the average fare charged to people coming into your town. Who was charged the most, people from your town, other towns, or villages?
4 What type of person uses the buses most frequently?
5 What comments did people make about the bus service?

Where Travellers Come From

Patterns of Housing

Most people in Britain live in towns. Only about one quarter of the population lives in the countryside. Over the last 150 years, more people have moved to the towns. The towns have become bigger and bigger as more houses are built. Today they show a mixture of housing styles. Older houses tend to be nearer the centre, with newer houses in the suburbs.

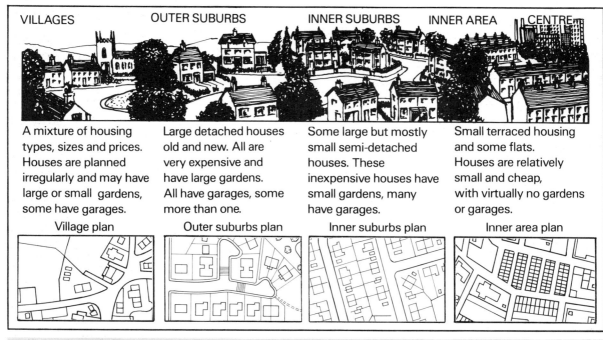

VILLAGES   OUTER SUBURBS   INNER SUBURBS   INNER AREA   CENTRE

A mixture of housing types, sizes and prices. Houses are planned irregularly and may have large or small gardens, some have garages.

Large detached houses old and new. All are very expensive and have large gardens. All have garages, some more than one.

Some large but mostly small semi-detached houses. These inexpensive houses have small gardens, many have garages.

Small terraced housing and some flats. Houses are relatively small and cheap, with virtually no gardens or garages.

Village plan   Outer suburbs plan   Inner suburbs plan   Inner area plan

Activities

A **1** In which plan above are the houses and streets closest together? Count the number of houses that you can see in each plan.

    2 What do you notice about the amount of garden space houses have, the further you travel from the town centre?

    3 From looking at the plans, say in which area you think it would be most interesting to live. What are your reasons?

    4 Suggest in which area you are most likely to find these houses:

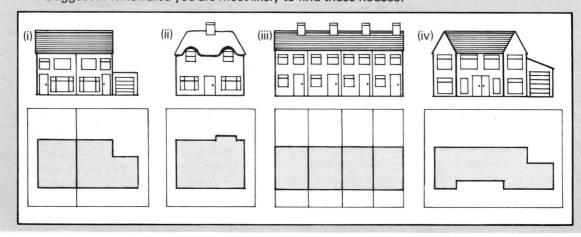

(i)   (ii)   (iii)   (iv)

Urban renewal is the replacement of older areas in towns by new estates. This complicates the housing patterns and often hides the way in which our towns have grown. In villages the pattern of growth is easier to see, as many older buildings are left undisturbed.

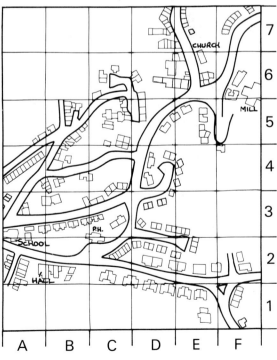

B 1 Name the types of housing that can be seen in squares A4, D1 and F2.
2 Where do you think are the oldest and the newest houses?
3 If you could live anywhere in the village, where would you choose?
4 Everyone has different ideas of their ideal home. Draw a picture of your ideal home.
5 List ten reasons why people might choose to live in the countryside or in a town. Think about transport, jobs, entertainment and age.

Things to think about
More people are choosing to live away from the centre of towns. Why do you think this is? What sort of things would you consider if you wanted to move to a different house and area?

Investigating
Housing Patterns

On average people move house every seven years. There are many reasons for moving home. People may move to a new job or they may want a larger home or to change from a flat to a house. One of the best ways to buy and sell a house is by advertising in the local newspaper.

The type of house people move to depends upon many things, especially the size of the family and the amount of money available. Here is an extract from a local newspaper. Each Thursday the paper has several pages set aside for advertising houses.

Newspaper adverts are a good source for finding out about the local patterns of housing. Look at a page of your local newspaper dealing with house sales. For each house, find out its location (street or area), type (detached, semi-detached or terraced) and its price. Enter your findings on a chart like this.

Address	Type	Type Symbol	Price	Price Symbol
48 Lee Road, NEWTON, Bradley	Semi-detached	◯	£31,000	M
'The Gables', ECTON	Detached	☐	£55,000	H
13 Bridge Street, THORNCLIFFE, Bradley	Terraced	◇	£15,000	L
6 Ash Terrace, THORNCLIFFE, Bradley	Terraced	◇	£16,950	L
27 Wood Avenue, LONGSHAW, Bradley	Semi-detached	◯	£22,500	M
Woodview Cottage, High Street, HARTON	Terraced	◇	£35,950	M
'Woodlands' WESTON, Bradley	Detached	☐	£62,250	H
'Valley View' High Street, HARTON	Semi-detached	◯	£29,950	M
12 Thorpe Grove, WESTFIELD, Bradley	Semi-detached	◯	£27,000	M
'Willow House', Stavley Road, MARSDEN, Bradley	Detached	☐	£70,000	H
6 Long Lane, EAST MORLEY	Detached	☐	£41,000	H
'Longdale', High Street, HARTON	Detached	☐	£55,500	H

Activities

1 Copy out the map below of Bradley and surrounding area. It is divided into four zones: the centre, inner suburbs, outer suburbs and villages.

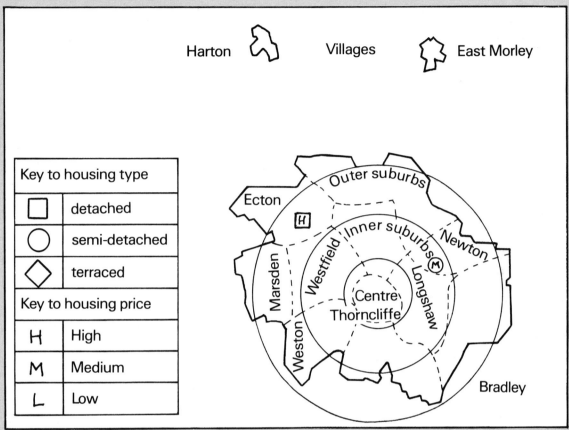

Key to housing type

☐	detached
○	semi-detached
◇	terraced

Key to housing price

H	High
M	Medium
L	Low

2 For each house listed in the survey chart put the correct house type and price symbols on the correct part of the map. The first two in Ecton and Newton have been done for you.

3 In which of the four zones are most terraced houses, and where are most detached and semi-detached houses?

4 In which areas are most high, medium and low price houses? What can you say about the price of houses in the town, as you move away from the centre?

5 Which area shows the greatest variety of house type and price?

6 Try the investigation yourself and answer the questions again using the results for your local area.
How does your map compare with the map above?
How many different estate agents advertised in your local newspaper?

Changing Patterns

Take a look outside the window. Perhaps someone is painting their house, or building an extension. The view might look much the same as it did last week or last month, but it is slowly changing. Over a number of years, an area might change so much that you would not recognise it as being the same place.

Activities

A Look at these photographs. They show the same street, but taken 80 years apart.

1 On a chart like this, record how transport, buildings and people have changed since 1905.

2 Draw sketches of each photograph. Clearly label the main changes that have taken place.

B The chart on page 27 shows the population changes in part of Northamptonshire from 1951 to 1981.

1 Work out the population change for each settlement.

2 Put the settlements into three lists, those that you think have grown quickly, those that you think have grown slowly, and those that have declined over this time.

3 On a copy of the map, colour the quickly-growing settlements in red, slowly-growing settlements in orange, and declining settlements in green.

4 Is there any difference between settlements near Northampton and those further away?

	1905	Today
Transport		
Buildings		
People		

	1951	1981
Northampton	104,432	157,217
Moulton	2,398	3,048
Brixworth	1,508	3,007
Silverstone	1,052	1,365
Harlestone	483	336
Wootton	1,115	1,952
Helmdon	551	693
West Haddon	704	858
Yardley Hastings	812	637
Cottesbrooke	206	158
Sywell	383	769

West Haddon ○   ○ Cottesbrooke

○   Brixworth ○

Moulton ○   ○ Sywell

Harlestone ○

NORTHAMPTON ○

Wootton ○

Yardley ○ Hastings

○ Helmdon

○ Silverstone

To see how villagers themselves have changed, we can look at Census Returns. Comparing information on the types of employment villagers were involved in and where they were born, can be very interesting.

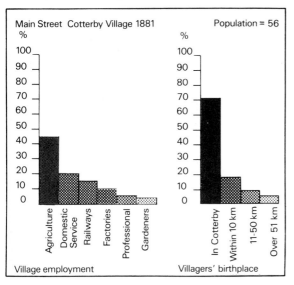

Main Street Cotterby Village 1881   Population = 56

Village employment

Villagers' birthplace

Main Street 1981	Population = 68	
Employment		**Birthplace**
agriculture	7 (10%)	in Cotterby 32 (47%)
professional	14 (21%)	within 10 km 19 (28%)
railways	9 (13%)	11-50 km 9 (13%)
factories	26 (38%)	over 51 km 8 (12%)
office/clerical	12 (18%)	

C 1 Use the information from 1981 to draw two new bar graphs.
2 Write a few sentences for each graph, describing the changes that have taken place.
3 Which jobs have died out since 1881?
4 What has happened to the number of people born and living in the village?

If people want to build houses, in either towns or villages, 'planning permission' from the local council has to be obtained. The council must make sure that buildings of architectural or historical interest are preserved and that new buildings fit in.

D 1 Do you think it is important to preserve old houses?
2 Can you think of any houses in your area that look out of place? Why don't they seem to fit in?

Investigating
Changing Patterns

When you get home, look out of your window into the street. Can you find out how your street has changed since it was built? Look at each house in turn, and at the street in general, and fill in a chart like this. Look at about five houses including your own.

Street name **Wood Grove**

Recorder **Sarah Wilson**

House Number	Changes in last month	Changes between 1 month and 1 year	Changes over 1 year ago
82	—	One new window frame. New roof	T.V. aerial, garage, dormer window
84	Painted fence	—	T.V. aerial
86	Two new window frames. Painted garage	New fence	New roof, T.V. aerial, garage
88	New gutter	Patio built. Replaced some roof tiles	T.V. aerial
85 (my house)	—	New front door. Painted front of house	T.V. aerial, new window frames, garage, greenhouse
Wood Grove	—	Re-surfaced the road	Lamp post, telephone box, bus stop, telegraph poles

Activities

A
1 When did the greatest changes occur, within a month, a year, or over a year ago?
2 Which house has changed the most since it was built?

B
1 Now investigate change in your street.
2 List the changes you found.
3 Has your street and its houses changed very much since it was built?
4 Draw a picture of your home. Colour in red the changes that have occurred since it was built.

New uses for old buildings

Many old buildings in your area may look more or less the same as they did when they were first built, but nowadays they may have different uses. By looking at an old shopping area, we can see how our area has changed.

Conduct an investigation in a local, old shopping area. On a prepared outline map like the one below, mark in the use of each building as you walk along the street. Note what each shop is selling and its address.

On your return to school, collect building use information from street directories of a chosen date, for comparison with your survey results. You may find that the numbers of shops and houses, and even their addresses have changed.

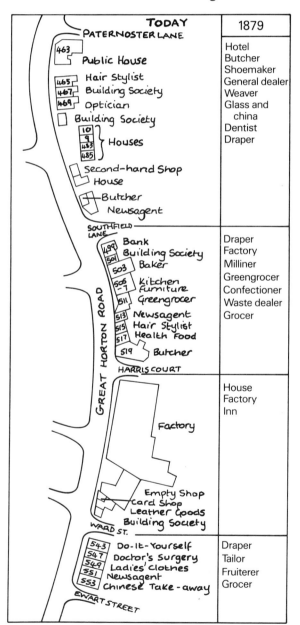

TODAY	1879
PATERNOSTER LANE	
463 Public House	Hotel
465 Hair Stylist	Butcher
467 Building Society	Shoemaker
469 Optician	General dealer
Building Society	Weaver
10, 9, 483, 485 Houses	Glass and china
	Dentist
	Draper
Second-hand Shop	
House	
Butcher	
Newsagent	
SOUTHFIELD LANE	
499 Bank	Draper
501 Building Society	Factory
503 Baker	Milliner
505-7 Kitchen Furniture	Greengrocer
511 Greengrocer	Confectioner
513 Newsagent	Waste dealer
515 Hair Stylist	Grocer
517 Health Food	
519 Butcher	
HARRIS COURT	
	House
	Factory
Factory	Inn
Empty Shop	
Card Shop	
Leather Goods	
Building Society	
WARD ST.	
543 Do-It-Yourself	Draper
547 Doctor's Surgery	Tailor
549 Ladies' Clothes	Fruiterer
551 Newsagent	Grocer
553 Chinese Take-away	
EWART STREET	

(GREAT HORTON ROAD runs along the left side)

C Look at the results for part of Great Horton Road in Bradford.
1 Copy and complete the chart below.
2 Plot the information from the completed chart on two bar graphs.
3 What do you notice when you compare them?
4 Which shops are there today which you would not have found in 1879?
5 Your local library may have some photographs of the survey area taken many years ago. Borrow some if you can and compare them with modern ones taken from the same position. Make some notes about the changes you can see.

	Today	1879
Food Shops	6	6
Clothes shops		
Banks, post offices, etc.		
Furnishings		
Others		
Houses		
Public Buildings		
Industry		
TOTAL		

Sample Worksheet

	Where do you live? (road, district- town)	How did you get here?	How often do you shop here?	Why do you shop here instead of locally?
	Supermarket name 'Save-it'- Westford Recorder's name Jane and Winston			
Interview 1	Sherwood Road Eastfield	Car	Every week	Cheaper
Interview 2	Telbrook	Car	Every two weeks	Large selection
Interview 3	Park Road Moor Green	Walk	Every week	Close by
Interview 4	Willow Lane Sheldon	Bus	Every week	Cheaper
Interview 5	Langton	Car	Twice a week	Pleasant surroundings

How does the supermarket help to make life easier for the shopper? Tick off any of these things that you find and add to them if you come across any more.

- ✓ car park
- ✓ cheque cashing service
- information desk
- ✓ serve yourself vegetables

- ✓ toilets
- restaurant/cafe
- ✓ late night shopping (after 6 pm)
- ✓ disabled shopper checkout.

Write down the names and prices of about ten everyday shopping items. Later compare these with a local shop.

'Bright Toothpaste'	54p
'Country Peas'	19p
'Sunrise Cereals'	64p
'Budget Coffee'	£1·20
1 kg apples	48p

10 fish fingers	64p
'Crisp Crackers'	32p
'Smith's Biscuits'	30p
½ kg bananas	41p
'East's Tinned Pears	43p

Notes for Teachers

AIMS   This book aims to:

- provide stimulus material which will lead children into studying their environment;
- develop the skills and concepts listed below through direct observation, practical investigation and information gathering and sorting;
- develop powers of deduction so that patterns of land use can be interpreted from visual evidence;
- suggest ideas so that opinions can be formed as to why settlements have been built in a particular way;
- provide a background vocabulary and knowledge from which to do this.

SKILLS   The book helps children to develop skills in:

- recognising types of homes and their representation on large-scale maps;
- conducting field surveys in order to gather information;
- making and using simple land use maps;
- aerial photograph interpretation;
- identifying similarity and difference in settlements and settlement patterns;
- gaining a balanced view of the available evidence and avoiding an over-commitment to only one explanation of it.

CONCEPTS   The book leads children towards developing concepts about:

- links between size of settlements and the services provided;
- the location of houses in relation to people's needs and preferences;
- transport patterns;
- the variety of urban and rural land use;
- continuity and change in housing habits;
- the complex nature of settlement growth.

ATTITUDES AND VALUES   The work in this book should foster:

- an attitude of curiosity which prompts enquiry into why settlements have grown in specific ways;
- a willingness to change a point of view in the face of evidence and a readiness to suspend a conclusion when information gathered shows inconsistency or lack of general pattern;
- a desire to probe more deeply for reasons and explanations and not merely to accept an unsubstantiated thought;
- an attitude which accepts differences in interpretations which in turn provoke reflection on observations and further thinking on the issues;
- an awareness of the aesthetic quality of our towns and villages and the need for respect for and conservation of our built environment generally.

Implementation

USING THIS BOOK   Each section provides sufficient material to allow work to be undertaken solely from the book. Using the ideas and material in these pages, teachers can lead children into investigations and interpretations immediately in the classroom. However, the intention is that children should venture out into their own environment and pursue the kind of research that the different sections suggest. Background vocabulary and classification knowledge is given so that children can move into the essence of their work directly and without the distractions and frustrations that field-work can so often incur.

MIXED ABILITY
The work is designed to cater for children of all abilities working in the same class. The information given is of easy readability and the tasks and field techniques suggested are clear and straightforward. The development of the investigations allows active participation by the least able, whilst the most able children are led into very challenging situations. Theories and hypotheses are usually neither right nor wrong, rather there are solutions which are more or less acceptable depending upon the quality and reliability of the evidence and the judgement upon which they are based. The better the evidence then the stronger the work will be. It is of great educational value if children can themselves find evidence to support their view but at the same time be aware of any weaknesses, shortcomings and inconsistencies in it.

At all ability levels children should be encouraged throughout this work to seek out patterns of: (i) similarity and difference; (ii) continuity and change; (iii) cause and effect.

PAGE BY PAGE

6 and 7 The Amenity Index can be measured using paces, time or distance. In advance of calculating their Index, the children can mark in their closest amenities on a personal map; this will aid in the calculation of distances.

8 and 9 A collection of photographs of various land uses around the school catchment area may be a useful introduction to this theme.

10 and 11 A separate plan, to be coloured in later, is valuable in both the investigations. Paper plans do not tend to travel well in the field, and the land uses recorded may be difficult to remove prior to colouring.

14 and 15 Permission will have to be sought from the management prior to the supermarket survey.

20 and 21 The traffic flow investigation should be carried out at three separate points along a main road; if possible, each point about one kilometre apart.
This survey is best conducted as group work, but the whole class can work at the same time at the same survey point, if necessary.
Permission will have to be obtained prior to conducting the bus station survey.

24 and 25 If the section in the local newspaper devoted to house sales is very long, it can be divided between the class. Several copies of the same issue will be needed. The price of houses is subject to regional variation and the price categories may need to be adjusted accordingly.

26 – 29 Comparison of local old and new photographs from the same position, provides a good introduction to this theme. More interest can be added to the first investigation if reminiscences concerning the street can be collected. Census returns are a useful source of information.
Old street directories, such as Kelly's, will provide the information necessary for the investigation on page 29.

Consultation with many teachers and advisers has revealed the need for a series which helps to structure topic work in the local environment. Structured investigations into the child's own environment can be a rich source of ideas and motivation leading to work in other disciplines. Each book in the series has the following aims:

● to provide sufficient information and structure **for pupils, either individually or in groups,** to carry out their own investigations into their environment;

● to provide, **for those pupils who are unable to go outside the classroom**, sufficient information for them to be able to experience the key ideas concerning the local environment;

● to provide **for the teacher** a set of structured ideas for investigating the environment.